Series title: **BLACK LEADERS IN THE FREEDOM STRUGGLE**

MARCUS GARVEY

by Marie Stuart

Illustrated by Folake Shoga

This book is part of a series written by Marie Stuart (Tyrwhitt) and published in her memory.

Marie wanted stories about the lives of these brave people to be more widely known. She believed that such stories would serve to encourage those facing the same challenges today.

Published in 1991 by East and Central Bristol Adult Continuing Education©, Bristol, with the sponsorship of the County of Avon and relatives, friends and colleagues of Marie Tyrwhitt.

Reprinted in 2003, 2005

Computer generated text and artwork by Alan Bain.

Distributors; Avanti Books, Unit 9, The iO Centre, Whittle Way, Arlington Business Park, Stevenage, SG1 2BD.

Printed by Printing & Stationery Services, UWE, Bristol.

Marie Stuart, the author of the books in the Black Leaders in the Freedom Struggle series, was a teacher of adults and children and a writer throughout all her long life. She was also a learner and one who believed that to be really alive means to be growing and changing. To do so means that we must be free. Free to question and free to find our own answers and our own way.

Marie Stuart wrote these books out of a passion for freedom for all, regardless of race, colour or creed, and out of a deep admiration for the heroes celebrated in this series. They are 'heroes' not because they conquered great empires, but because, by their actions and their example, they gave something of great value to the liberation of their people. They stood up and took their place proudly amongst the human race, having struggled heroically against the disadvantages to which they were born. These stories and those lives will never die as long as we have the courage to strive for our human right to dignity and equality and the generosity to realise that the breath of freedom is sharing. It is in that spirit that these books should be read and in loyalty to the memory of those brave black leaders in our freedom struggle.

MARCUS MOSIAH GARVEY (1887-1940)

Chapter One

"I shall teach the black man to see beauty in himself."

Who was Marcus Garvey? The reply Martin Luther King made to that question was, "He was the first man ... to give millions of Negroes a sense of dignity and destiny."

Slavery had been abolished in Jamaica long before Marcus was born, but the black people who lived there were still suffering from the bad effects it left behind. In those days the whites were looked up to as superior beings, the masters. If a black man had a light skin he felt proud of it. As Marcus grew up he had to decide whether to go along with the 'black-whites,' or to help improve the status of the black people. He said, "I choose the latter. I shall teach the black man to see beauty in himself." That is what his life's work was all about.

He was born in St. Ann's Bay, Jamaica, on August 17th, 1887. He was the youngest of eleven children. His second Christian name was meant to be Moses, but he was christened Marcus Mosiah. His parents were poor and, as a child, he knew what it was like to go hungry. He was able to attend an elementary school and he learnt quickly. He used to play with the four children of a clergyman who lived nearby, but then the time came for the two girls to be sent away to a school in Edinburgh, Scotland. Before they left home they were told by their father that they must never write or try to get in touch with Marcus again, "because he was a 'nigger.' " He was deeply hurt by this insult and never forgot it. It was his first bitter lesson in racism.

He had to leave school at the age of fourteen and was sent by his father to Kingston to work in the printing trade. What he learnt there during the next few years was very helpful to him when he began writing and editing newspapers later on. Also, the talks he had with journalists in the National Club made him aware of the world outside of the island of Jamaica. He wanted to travel and see things for himself.

With the help of an uncle, he got a job as a time-keeper on a plantation in Costa Rica. He was shocked when he saw how the migrant workers were exploited by the managers. He wrote about it to the British Consul who replied that he could do nothing. So he went to Panama where he found things just as bad. He wrote more letters and articles about these conditions and had some of them published, but they had no effect. It was the same story in all the other Central American countries he went to. Then he read an article in one of the National Club's newspapers which said:

"The coloured and black people in Jamaica can only hope to better their conditions by uniting with the coloured and black people of the United States of America and with the other West Indian Islands, and indeed with all the Negroes in all parts of the world."

These words were a torch to him. They showed him the way to get rid of all the misery he had seen on his travels. But he knew he was too young and inexperienced. He felt he needed to know more. He needed to prepare himself for what he was beginning to feel was his life's mission. First he had to get ready intellectually, emotionally and spiritually - "for no man can advance beyond his preparation."

He had a sister living in England and he wrote to her to ask if she could help him. She generously sent him his fare and invited him to come over. He soon found work in the docks of London, Cardiff, and Liverpool. There he talked to and made friends with African and West Indian seamen who were very useful to him in his work later on.

Marcus spent most of his time in London where he met African students who had come over to study at the University. They lent him their books and took him to some of the lectures. He learned from them something about the history of Africa. They had long talks, discussions and arguments late into the night. He also became very friendly with an Egyptian journalist who taught him about the history of Egypt and its greatness in the past. It was through Ali's help that Marcus was able to get some of his articles published in the *African Times* and *Orient Express.*

While he was in London, he came across Booker Washington's book, *Up From Slavery.* He bought a copy of it and read it with great interest. Booker, who had been a slave himself, was then head of an Agricultural and Industrial Institute called Tuskegee, in the South Belt of the U.S.A. His students were all black and had either been slaves or were the children of slaves, Marcus made up his mind to visit the Institute and talk with Booker when he returned.

It was now June, 1914, just before the outbreak of the First World War in Europe. Garvey was coming up to his twenty-seventh birthday, and he felt that he was ready to start putting some of his ideas into practice. But first he had to work for his return passage.

All the way over on the ship he was thinking about what he had learned from his African friends. He was black, as they were, yet he had never been to Africa. Now he was going back to Jamaica where there were more black men than white. The blacks were all Negroes. Some of the old ones had been slaves and had been born in Africa. Africa was their home-land. The others, like himself, had never seen it. "So where," he asked himself, "is *their* country? Where is the Black Man's government? Where is his king and his kingdom? Where is his president? His ambassador? His army? His navy? His men of big affairs? He could not find them and so he said, "I will help to make them."

Amy Ashwood

Chapter Two

UNIA - a New Movement for the Dignity of Black People

Garvey's mind was full of plans and within a few days of his arrival back in Kingston he set to work to organise a committee. On August 1st, 1914, the U.N.I.A. was born. The initials stood for the Universal Negro Improvement and Conservation Association - UNIA. August 1st was Emancipation Day, the anniversary of the day when slaves in the Caribbean had been freed seventy-six years previously, so it had a special meaning for Garvey and all those who were in tune with his ideals. He was elected President, and Amy Ashwood was the Secretary. Amy was later to become Garvey's wife.

A list of general aims for the Society was drawn up, ready for when it spread to other countries. The special local Jamaican aims were worded as follows:

1. To establish educational and industrial colleges for the further education of our boys and girls.

2. To redeem the fallen and degraded (especially the criminal class).

3. To administer to and assist the needy.

4. To promote a better taste for commerce and industry.

5. To promote a universal confraternity and strengthen the bonds of brotherhood and unity among the races.

6. To help in the development of the country.

These objectives were very much in line with Booker Washington's Institute in Tuskegee, and Garvey intended to use this as his model for a similar one in Jamaica. He wrote to Booker about it and planned to visit him to see how the school was run. Unfortunately Booker died before it could be finally arranged.

Booker's aim had been to bring about racial harmony. It would be the next step forward after Freedom had been declared in America at the end of the bitterly fought Civil War. In Jamaica, a British Colony, slavery had been abolished in 1838, and yet eighty years later the black people were still oppressed by their poverty. It was said that the labouring conditions had been arranged by the original employers to keep the people as near as possible to the condition of slavery.

Garvey was coming to the belief that a stronger line needed to be taken if their situation was to be improved.

When Marcus went to the U.S.A. in 1916, he wanted to visit Tuskegee and raise funds for a setting up a similar Institute in Jamaica. However, when he showed a friend the letter he had received from Booker just before his death, the friend replied that he did not think Jamaica needed a Tuskegee, but that something more radical was needed. He introduced Garvey to some journalists and gave him a list of leading men in New York and other cities who would be able to help him. So Garvey travelled around America to find out what was really happening there. He had planned to go straight back to Jamaica, but instead he went to New York.

There, in Harlem, the black area of New York, he found that nearly a thousand members had been enrolled in UNIA. He felt that it would be wiser for him to make his headquarters there as it would give him greater scope than Kingston, Jamaica, could offer. So he went to live with a Jamaican family in Harlem and earned his living working as a printer.

He also wrote articles for a newspaper called *Negro World* and went around making speeches to get people to know about UNIA. Setting up a big organization costs money and he had very little. Often he went hungry. He sometimes felt so faint for want of food that he fell off the soap-box while making a speech! With all the walking that he had to do, his shoes got worn out and let in the wet. He caught colds and ended up in hospital with pneumonia. Yet more and more people came to listen to him. He had the gift of oratory and could make an audience laugh, cry, applaud, hiss or cheer as he wished. His speeches were taken down in shorthand as there were no tape recorders in those days. It took two people to keep up with him as he spoke quickly. Here are the words from one of the speeches he made in Jamaica:

"I am here to give you, if I can, a new spirit of manhood. Not the spirit to bow and cringe, to apologise, but the spirit to strike forward for the rights of the Negro people of the world. I, like the majority of you, was born in this country, circumvented by the conditions of the country - the environment of this country that sits on the black man - that he must be merely a hewer of wood and a carrier of water - a servant looking up to the white man as a superior and master - who was born to believe himself inferior to other races - born not to have hope for himself. Under this environment which keeps a black man at the foot of the ladder, I was as entitled to climb as any other man, be he white, yellow or black."

This was the theme that Garvey used in many of his speeches. His idea was to encourage his listeners to make an effort to 'walk tall,' to take a pride in their race instead of passively accepting that it was their lot to be the underdogs. He also wanted them to feel that Africa was a mighty continent and that, even if they never went there, it was their homeland and they should be proud of it.

So, although he had gone to America with the idea of following in the footsteps of Booker Washington, he changed from being a reformist to becoming a Black Nationalist. He urged his listeners to join the world-wide movement to "promote the intellectual, social, commercial, industrial and national interest of the down-trodden race" of which they were members. And they responded. They came in their thousands to listen to his speeches and join UNIA. He was the right man in the right place at the right time.

Chapter Three

Garvey's Movement seen as a Threat

As America was now fighting in the European World War, many factories had been set up in the North and workers were needed for them. Thousands of the very poor ex-slaves from the South migrated to the North to fill these jobs. Those who went to New York went to Harlem, the Negro area, and they heard Garvey's speeches and joined UNIA. As they now had money to spend, Garvey urged them to buy bonds and stamps in the company's Liberty Loan Drives. The Negro Factories Corporation was set up and ran co-operative grocery stores, restaurants, a steam laundry, a tailoring and dressmaking shop, a millinery store and a publishing house. UNIA members were employed in running all these enterprises and factories. The idea was "to build and operate big industrial centres in the United States, Central America, the West Indies and Africa to manufacture every marketable commodity." Garvey did not own these factories personally, or make any money for himself out of them. They were all owned by UNIA. In a way, they were a development of Booker Washington's idea of the black people being self-sufficient.

The after-effect of the war in Europe, however, had a very ugly side, as it led to an increase in bouts of racism. During the conflict three hundred and seventy thousand black people had been called upon to serve in the American armed forces. Many of these men had given their lives in the fight for 'Democracy,' but those who returned found that, instead of being thanked and looked upon as heroes, they were treated like dirt. They were useful as 'cannon fodder' but not wanted as equal citizens. There were race riots, lynchings, and the Klu Klux Klan began its horrific work. Garvey soon decided that the Tuskegee model was not the answer to this problem. He wrote in one of his newspapers that "the Negro, through UNIA, is *demanding the right* and taking unto himself the *power* to control his own destiny." These words made governments sit up and take notice. This man, Garvey, was becoming dangerous. He must be watched.

Meanwhile the membership of UNIA was increasing daily. When it started in Harlem, it had eight branches, the largest with fifty members. Within a few months it had thousands of supporters all over the country. It was like a rising tide. The movement did not rely only on members attending committee meetings. Garvey knew how to appeal to the general public and to the young. For these, UNIA was like a huge club. It became their whole way of life. Couples met through it, got married and had families. In New York, the Society even arranged to issue its own birth certificates, in addition to the State registration.

Garvey was the leader, but the movement was now too vast for one person to be in charge of everything. There were many branches with active supporters running pre-school play groups, Sunday Schools and Night Schools. Here, children and young people were taught ,about the lives of black people who had worked for the freedom of the slaves - people such as Harriet Tubman, Sojourner Truth, Frederick Douglass and others. 'Uncle Tom's Cabin' was a set book which they had to read. Garvey also wrote poems for them to learn and recite aloud. The children were given black dolls. They were all shown pictures of black angels and a black Madonna and Christ. They were educated and encouraged to have good manners. They were not 'street kids.' Mothers used Garvey's name to teach the children to behave by saying, "Mr.Garvey wouldn't like you to do that," or "Mr. Garvey will be pleased if you do this."

Garvey was very particular about the importance of UNIA members paying attention to their physical appearance. Since all the ex-slaves had grown up in cabins with no wash-basins or bathrooms, and even the slums of Harlem were no better, it was not easy for them to wash themselves or their clothes. He would tell them, "You keep yourselves clean, then you can earn the respect of the white man. I know some of *them* are filthy, but that is no excuse for you. It doesn't matter if you have only one shirt and one pair of trousers; wash them. You can get a penny soap. The sun doesn't charge you for drying them. If you haven't got an iron, you can put your trousers under your mattress at night and by the morning they'll have something of a crease." He taught them to take a pride in themselves. He would never allow advertisements for 'hair straighteners' or 'face bleaches' in his newspapers. For him, to pretend not to be a Negro was to let the race down. It was as if they despised their own appearance, and that was part of their slave legacy which they must get rid of. He taught black men and women to see beauty in themselves.

One of his ways of doing this was by holding parades through the streets of Harlem. They were magnificent spectacles. Each branch wore its own uniform. That of the Africa Legion was black with gold braid on the sleeves of the jacket, with green or red buttons and embroidered epaulettes. Their black trousers had a red stripe down each leg and their caps had gold workings. The officers carried dress swords and some rode horse-back. The ranks had guns which were exact copies of real ones, except that these carbines were sealed so that they could not be fired. Nevertheless, they looked very impressive. Then there were the Black Cross

Nurses, the Universal Africa Motor Corps, the Black Eagle Flying Corps (on motor bikes). There were bands and choirs singing Garvey's Freedom Songs. Thousands of citizens would gather just to see them pass, but only black UNIA members were allowed to join the procession.

Chapter Four
UNIA becomes International

In 1920 it was decided to hold an International UNIA Convention. Again, August 1st was the opening day. Two thousand delegates came from twenty-five countries and four continents, for the movement was now getting known all over the world. After a huge procession through the streets of Harlem, twenty-five thousand people packed into Madison Square Gardens to hear Garvey's opening speech in which he told them:

"We shall organize the four hundred million Negroes of the world into a vast organization to plant the banner of freedom on the great continent of Africa. If Europe is for the Europeans, then Africa is for the black people of the world."

Garvey was the Provisional President of Africa and the President General of UNIA. Other leaders were given such titles as "Knight of the Nile, Earl of the Congo, Viscount of the Niger, Baron Zambesi." They had splendid robes of office. Garvey himself wore a gown of purple, green and gold and an academic cap. The whole affair was like a glorious pageant to boost the morale of a down-trodden people. The pomp and splendour was a deliberate attempt to attract attention and recruit more followers.

A flag was unfurled amid cheers and shouts and thereafter became the UNIA symbol. It had three stripes - red, black and green. The red stood for the blood which had been shed by the people, the black for the Negro race, the green for the new hopeful life of future generations. A 'Declaration of the

Rights of the Negro People of the World' was drafted. The fifty-four listed 'rights' were all dealing with such things as 'political and judicial equality' and set out a broad programme of Black Nationalism. Among other things, it objected to the education system which taught black children to think of the white people as superior to the black race. The motto they adopted was "One God, One Aim, One Destiny." Altogether, the Convention was a tremendous success.

Garvey now claimed that the organization had two million members and he started a weekly paper called "The Negro World." It was printed in French and Spanish as well as English. Garvey used its pages to spread his ideas. He told people about the past glories of Egypt and of the heroism of such men as Paul Bogle and Toussaint L'Ouverture who had led slave rebellions. He urged the present black generation to get up and fight against racism and win their own rights.

He thought of a clever plan to have his newspapers delivered all over the world. He had many Caribbean friends amongst the seamen he had met when he worked in the docks in England. He now asked these men to hand out his paper freely at ports where they docked. They would say, "Here, take this and read it and when you've finished, pass it on. It's important. Read it!" And they did. Those who could not read asked those who could to read it to them. Some learned whole passages by heart and re-told them to people who lived in remote areas. In this way, many people in distant parts of the world - Africa, India, even Japan, got to know about Garvey and what UNIA stood for. Some of the present day leaders in Africa first got to know about his ideas in this way and were influenced by them. The seamen, who delivered the papers for him, did not want to be paid because they agreed with him. They wanted to help get his message across. Later on, when some of the colonial powers got wise to what was happening, they tried to put a stop to it by banning the paper and making it illegal to possess a copy. In one country it was even punishable by death, but as the seamen were always moving from one port to another, it was not easy to stop them.

Besides writing articles for this newspaper, Garvey made many speeches. With contributions from supporters, UNIA was now able to buy a large auditorium in Harlem which they called Liberty Hall. This became their headquarters where members were able to meet and make plans.

There were now large numbers of unemployed black people in Harlem as the European War had ended (in 1918) and those who had answered their country's call for workers during the 'war effort' were no longer needed. There were also two hundred thousand black soldiers who had been demobbed and were now without work. They had fought to 'make the world safe for democracy' but had come back to the old caste-system and a state of near-slavery. They flocked to hear Garvey's speeches. In one of them he said:

"My opponents say I am against white and fair-skinned people. This is not so. I am against the class system here which keeps the poor man down, and the poor are mostly black people. It is only natural, therefore, that their interest should be nearest and dearest to my heart."

But was that enough? Clearly not. He needed *power* to help them as well as heart, because, as he had said in one of his other speeches, "A country without land is a country without power."

He talked things over with other members of the Committee and they decided to move the headquarters of UNIA to Africa. Some of the money which had been collected was used to buy land from the Liberian government in West Africa and the dream-plan was to settle some of the UNIA leaders and their supporters there with Garvey as their elected President. When they heard of it, the French, English and United States were all against the idea. Even at the time Garvey wrote:

"It is a mistake to suppose I want to take all the Negroes to Africa. I believe they have a perfect right to live in the U.S. and aspire to equality of opportunities and treatment. But I foresee the building of a great state in Africa which, featuring in the concert of the great nations, will make the Negro as respectable as the others."

INCORPORATED UNDER THE LAWS OF THE STATE OF DELAWARE

BLACK STAR LINE, INC.

Chapter Five

The Black Star Line & Garvey's Ruin

Alas, it was a dream which sadly led to his ruin. He thought that if UNIA members wanted to visit Africa, and perhaps settle there, then they should have their own Steamship Line to take them there. As usual with him, to think of an idea was to carry it out. So the Black Star Line was launched.

It was to be owned and operated by black people to form a link between black nations all over the world. Thousands rushed to buy shares in the Company. Only black people could buy them and no-one could own more than two hundred. Each share cost five dollars, and a dollar was worth less then than now. In a short time there was enough money to buy three ships, but the whole venture was ill-fated from the start. Of course the White Star Line was opposed to it and 'big business' ganged up against it. For instance, supplies of coal were held up to delay sailing - these were the days of steam-ships. Also, all the sailors were black people, and lacked the experience of being in control. So in spite of high hopes, the Company went bankrupt in 1922. Sadly, this was the beginning of the end for Garvey.

However, Edgar Hoover, who later became the head of the Federal Bureau of Investigation in the U.S., welcomed the news. He had had his eyes on Garvey for a long time and had been hoping that he would commit some crime for which he could be deported. Garvey's socialist and anti-colonial views were against all that Hoover stood for. As yet, he had not been able to pin anything on him that fell foul of the law. Now the opportunity presented itself. Garvey could not be brought to trial for going bankrupt, but if it could be proved that he had "knowingly and with criminal intent" sent letters to advertise the sale of the Black Star stock, after he knew the Company was in a hopeless state, then he could be convicted. At his trial Garvey defended himself. He told the jury of his work for his race and ended his plea with the words:

"I stand before you and this Honourable Court for judgment and I do not regret what I have done for the Universal Negro Improvement Association, because I did it from the fullness of my soul. We had no monetary considerations but the good we could do for our race for this and succeeding generations."

As they waited for the verdict of the jury, many of Garvey's supporters were in tears. They felt that the evidence brought against him was trumped-up. It was an envelope which a man brought to court. He said that it contained a letter advertising the sale of Black Star stock after the Company had gone bankrupt. It took nine hours before the jury reached their decision of 'guilty.' Then the judge pronounced sentence: a fine of one thousand dollars and five years imprisonment. Garvey appealed against the verdict and, while he was waiting for the result, he heard that the Liberian government had pulled out of the bargain they had made with him, and that the U.S. Firestone Rubber Company had taken possession of all the equipment which had been subscribed for the venture. So the romantic dream had come to nothing and he was left in ruins. When he spoke about it after his release he said, "They dragged me through the streets of Harlem like a common thief," and tears rolled down his cheeks at the memory. However, his UNIA supporters did not blame him. For them, the Black Star Line was a symbol of what some day they might be able to accomplish even though it had failed. These words, spoken by a seventy year old Jamaican forty years after the event (and reported by the press in 1964) tell what the black people felt about it at the time:

"Garvey was the greatest thing to happen to a black man. I remember the day when his Black Star Line ship land at Beef Market Pier. I, me here, step up and look around, see black men piloting ship. That ship smash up after a while but see today, more black men building ship." - It was this spark that Garvey had been able to kindle in his countrymen that, once lit, would not be extinguished.

Chapter Six

Garvey's Triumphant Defeat

Garvey was released in 1927 after serving two years and nine months of his sentence, and was deported to his native land, Jamaica, never again to return to the U.S.A. He was accompanied by his second wife, Amy Jaques (his first marriage having ended in divorce). He was given a hero's welcome by his followers who rejoiced at his home-coming. However, one of the newspapers wrote at the time:

"We will not be surprised to find that Jamaica is meant to be his St. Helena on authority of a powerful combination whose interests some observers say is to keep Garvey down."

Perhaps it was to try to prove to himself and others that he would not be 'kept down' that he spent the next eighteen months travelling with his wife. First they set off on a Caribbean tour, but he found that he was not allowed to enter any of the Central American countries. Then the *Jamaica Times* reported that "the British Government seems still to fear him and has recently refused to grant him a passport for himself and his wife to go to British Guiana or any of the nearby islands."

Amy Jaques Garvey

Since he was banned from entry to the United States, Garvey was cut off from UNIA headquarters. This meant he could no longer make speeches in Liberty Hall in Harlem to make appeals for money for any new ideas. He even had to telegraph his weekly front page articles for the *Negro World.* To carry on his work as leader of UNIA he needed to be in a capital city; Kingston in Jamaica was too small and still a colonial city. So he decided to move to London with the intention of making it his headquarters, as he knew he had supporters there. He was disappointed at his reception. He made speeches in Hyde Park but he no longer drew crowds as of old. Then he hired the Albert Hall for a meeting but it was poorly attended. In the speech he made on that occasion he reminded his audience that the cotton which fed the mills of Lancashire had come from the slave plantations and that, therefore, some of the wealth of the British Empire had been contributed by black people. So he appealed to them for support for UNIA, but without much success.

Disappointed, they moved on to Paris and then to Geneva, where Garvey tried to bring the plight of the black people to the attention of the League of Nations. Again, he had no success, as he was not the representative of the whole African nation. Then they went to Canada but were not permitted to enter. Why were all these doors being shut against them? Why?

So he returned to Jamaica, saddened but not yet defeated. As one of the newspapers put it:

"His freedom abroad might be restricted by strong forces, but his basic ideas cannot possibly be destroyed - that dynamic force is at present in the island from which place he can operate with good effect."

And indeed he did, for he immediately set about forming a UNIA branch in Kingston, and made plans for a Convention to be held there, similar to those which had taken place in Harlem. As usual, the opening day was August 1st, but the year was now 1929. Delegates poured in from all over the United States and Central America. It was a case of, "if Mohammed cannot go to the mountain, then the mountain must come to Mohammed." People formed in a procession through the streets of Kingston such as had never been seen there before. By 9 a.m. the stadium was full to overflowing. This in itself was proof that UNIA still met the needs of masses of black people. It also showed that the organization was truly democratic since it had survived in strength during the years that Garvey had been in prison and on his travels since his release. His opening address showed that he had not lost any of his skill as an orator. He began:

"Although, as British Negroes, we were freed in 1838, and in America in 1865 from the chattel slavery, unfortunately we have still remained slaves; and the efforts of UNIA are to create a second emancipation - an emancipation of the minds and thoughts of four hundred million Negroes of the world."

The crowd cheered and cheered. Before they dispersed, they passed a resolution for the building of a new school. Nothing could have pleased Garvey more, for he was, like Booker Washington before him, a great believer in the value of education.

Until now, Garvey had not taken an active part in local politics because he did not want to tie himself down to everyday affairs. His vision was wider. He had looked upon himself as a leader for black people all over the world. Now his wings had been clipped. But he could not remain inactive. He looked around and saw that there were two Jamaicas: one was white, or near-white (the Mulattoes) and wealthy; the other, the majority, black and poor. The rich wore robes and had power; they were the judges, lawyers, doctors, teachers. The poor wore rags. So he went into politics.

As always, he identified with the black people and the poor people. He made a start by founding the People's Political Party (P.P.P.) and in his manifesto set forth many social and economic ideas far in advance of his time. He introduced the ideas of a minimum wage for all working classes and an eight hour day. He also wanted an All Island Water Board to bring water and drains to all houses; a Legal Aid Department to advise and protect those who could not afford the services of a lawyer; a university, a polytechnic, a national opera house, a race course, and a national park like Hyde Park in London. This was at a time when a black man could be employed to work from sunrise to sunset for one shilling and three pence a day, and a serving maid in a house from dawn till eleven o'clock at night for five shillings a week! As might have been expected, his enemies said (just as Joseph's brothers said of him), "Here comes the dreamer; let us kill him!"

He was asking for a social revolution and of course, the rich whites and Mulattoes opposed him. They did more. They fined him and had him imprisoned for three months for "Seditious Libel" because he had implied in his manifesto that some of the judges and lawyers were corrupt (which they were). So he lost the election. From the start, it was obvious that he had no chance of winning. The poor who would have voted for him in their thousands had no vote at the time, and those who could were against his socialist ideas.

He tried to fight back. He wrote articles for his own newspaper and for other papers that would print them. He set up a Workers' and Labourers' Association. He led a deputation to the Governor of the Island to try to make him aware of "the pitiful condition of the poor." He sent a petition to the King of England and Labour members of Parliament. This at least led to a Royal Commission being sent out to see what was happening in the West Indies. But by this time the struggle was getting too much even for his brave spirit. He told Amy Bailey, who had worked with him in UNIA from the beginning, "I left Jamaica a broken man, broken in spirit, broken in health, broken in pocket. I will never, never go back." And he never did.

He lived in poverty in a small flat in West Kensington, London. He was a defeated man. After suffering two strokes, he died in 1940. But his spirit still lives on. Many of the African leaders of today were influenced by his writings. Two hundred UNIA branches still exist in various parts of the world. It was Garvey's ideas which laid the foundation for the Black Power Movement.

Jamaica's former Prime Minster, Edward Seaga, had Garvey's body returned to Jamaica in 1964, with a twenty-one gun salute, to proclaim him their first national hero. This is what he said of him in the programme which was broadcast to commemorate Garvey's centenary:

"He was a man who understood the basic personality and psychology of the people, so he was able to mobilise them. He was not a great organizer or good manager, and that is where he failed. But he was perhaps the most outstanding person in the first half of the twentieth century."

Another tribute was paid to him in the same programme by Amy Bailey, then aged ninety-one, in these words:

"We had nothing, no-one, and here came this little Moses from somewhere in the Caribbean to tell us what we *were!*"

THE GARVEY SONG

Listen to the voice of Garvey, the Negroes' friend,
Garvey came to lead his people home again.
Four hundred million of humanity all unite,
Garvey came to lead his people home again.

Series title:
BLACK LEADERS IN THE FREEDOM STRUGGLE

Titles published

Sojourner Truth

Frederick Douglass

Josiah Henson

Harriet Tubman

Booker Washington

Marcus Garvey

Toussaint L'Ouverture

The Wonderful Adventures of Mrs Seacole

Paul Robeson

Martin Luther King

and an introduction: Slavery in America

Cassette tapes available:

Frederick Douglass
Marcus Garvey